BRAIN

THE UNIVERSITY OF GEORGIA PRESS ATHENS AND LONDON

LORD BRAIN

POEMS BY BRUCE BEASLEY

Published by the University of Georgia Press
Athens, Georgia 30602
© 2005 by Bruce Beasley
Designed by Mindy Basinger Hill
Set in 10.5/15 Minion
Printed and bound by Thomson-Shore
The paper in this book meets the guidelines for
permanence and durability of the Committee on
Production Guidelines for Book Longevity of the
Council on Library Resources.

Printed in the United States of America
09 08 07 06 05 P 5 4 3 2 1

Library of Congress Cataloging-in-Publication Data

Beasley, Bruce, 1958–
    Lord Brain : poems / by Bruce Beasley.
       p. cm. — (The contemporary poetry series)
    ISBN 0-8203-2730-1 (pbk. : alk. paper)
    1. Brain, W. Russell Brain (Walter Russell Brain), Baron,
       1895–1966—Poetry. 2. Neurosciences—Poetry.
       I. Title. II. Contemporary poetry series (University
       of Georgia Press)
    PS3552.E1748L67 2005
    811'.54—dc22   2005000962

British Library Cataloging-in-Publication Data available

*for Suzanne
and Jin,
because these
trillions of
synapses allow
me to love you*

As one
neurologist we
spoke
with put it,
"Ten billion
neurons,
10^{14} different
connections—
hell, you can
do anything
with that.
That's more
than enough
to contain a
'soul.'"

THE THREE-POUND UNIVERSE

JUDITH HOOPER AND DICK TERESI,

ONE

*wherein is traced
the way that
light dwelleth in
the brain . . .
& God moves
among the lobes
& through the
strobe lights,
& lightning
bugs consume
slugs, & the
soul is pineal
gland & filthy
window, & the
cosmos resists
disintegration
only because it
has no center,
& slices of living
brain are laid on
the examining
table*

THE EYE IS FORMED BY THE LIGHT FOR THE LIGHT

SO THAT THE INNER LIGHT MAY MEET THE OUTER. **GOETHE**

is crusted with oil paint in dull ivory, left vacuous as an undetected
   moon—

I frame no hypothesis
about gravity, Newton said, since
he could never discover a reason for it
in any phenomenon,

ye cause of gravity is what I do not pretend to know—

& Phineus Gage, when a three-foot iron tamping rod blasted
   through his eye socket
& frontal lobe, survived
intact & conscious & asked immediately for the rod, but was utterly
changed from within: foulmouthed, transient, loud, *a child*
in intellect but with the strong animal passions of a man, his Organs
   of Veneration & Benevolence
shredded, & his friends said *Gage is no longer Gage,*
& when he died they buried the iron rod

beside him, icon of his unspared & rescrambled soul—

For Aristotle the brain could do nothing but cool, the internal
rivers of its ventricles there only to wash

down & chill the fevered heart-blood—

& somewhere the scans of my father's ruptured brain stem & pons
wait to be refound in the wonder-cabinet of the Macon Hospital's
   archives
(Gage is no longer Gage)
Your daddy ain't gon come back alive, & he ain't gon die
my grandmother said, *his brain's all gone*
but the rest of him's here, he's gon live on & on in Intensive Care

4

till my uncle flew there in the night, on his private jet, said *Poor*
    bastard,
& let the respirator signal throb

off—

Augustine believed the soul was like a window, & sin
the smudges grown over it that scatter the light
of the divine so it withdraws & cannot open
a transparence of self to God, that undiffraction—

Narrow is the mansion of my soul—he said—*expand Thou it*—

This morning my window's
stuck with old spiderwebs rain-smushed into the glass, & smashed
gnats & ripped-off mothwings, & what wakelight
stabs through the gutter-drip of moss
gets dispelled by a smirch left by the first
sticky March pollen & the last

hundred-&-one-straight nights of rain—

I bought a light-box that blasts my eyes all winter, to fool
my pineal into thinking the days aren't sleet-dripped & fogbound—
Its ultraviolet photons sealed on my retina, white on white on white,
ten-thousand-lux counterfeit of sunlight to fool
my cortex out of searching for spectral
evidence of my own, & the universe's, insufficiency—
frantic fist-rubs on the soul, then: glass greased over with rain-
fog & the dull steam of my every

obfuscating breath—

Newton worried that the universe ought,
by all logic, to collapse
on itself, since gravity should haul everything inexorably together,
   helium
crushing carbon crushing manganese crushing light
—*& by consequence fall down to ye middle of the whole space & there
   compose one great spherical mass*—
& determined he could only justify *what is* if the cosmos
had no gravitational core
(*I frame no hypothesis*) being
infinite in all directions, so therefore

would have no "center" into which it *could* collapse—

like this wanting-to-disintegrate
spherical mass
of brain, a hundred
trillion synapses hiding—where?—a *self*

—more neurons inside my skull than humans who have ever lived—

& ye causes of all this brooding & inconsolation
& sudden convolutions of pleasure
I do not pretend to know
but can't stop hunting

down any way through these jellyfish-mucid lobes—

Haldane, when he wondered
about the temperature of the living brain
had a thermocoupling inserted up
through his own jugular, into the gray & tepid

matter in his skull—

toward the cortex, where the *thought* gets thought, where the *felt*
gets known-to-have-been felt,
as it wallows, folded & folded
in on itself, an eighth of an inch thick, depressions
& hillocks, gyri & sulci, hunches
& in-burrowing, washed-chill & uncenterable
gouge—decerebrated
rats stumbling through door

after exactly right door . . .

MELANCHOLIA ORACLES: I

Dead End sign, under strangle of plucked blackberry vines.
Root-wad bared, gnat- & bluefly-swarmed.
Chirr of cicadas perfectly timed to my expired breaths.
& a traffic hiss, insistent, far-off through the firs

& interior, sealed in, as if I could hear
the neurons' billions of little sizzles, their
scramble for the one perfect linkup,
that pattern of synaptic leaps that would make all this cohere—

IF RELIGIOUS BELIEFS ARE SIMPLY NEUROCOGNITIVE PROCESSES THAT REDUCE ANXIETY CONCERNING THE DISSOLUTION OF THE SENSE OF SELF

—M. A. Persinger, "Paranormal and Religious Beliefs May Be Mediated Differentially by Subcortical and Cortical Phenomenological Processes of the Temporal (Limbic) Lobes," *Perceptual and Motor Skills* (1993), 76, 247–51

Transtemporal,

under a motorcycle helmet & its four solenoids,
under its electrodes jabbed into the skin
& a daub of conducting gel, in a black vault,
the soundproof chamber in Persinger's lab
called The Dungeon, through

"the mesiobasal structures of the temporal lobes,"

a 10-mG magnetic field
stirs the neurons to burst-fire,
stirs a microseizure
in hippocampus & amygdala,
& there comes a presence
from out of the mute
right brain, who brings
"a sense of absolute meaningfulness to the cosmos"
("perhaps a species-
specific buffer

against death anxiety")—

Spike & slow-wave
on the EEG. There stirs
in the magnetized mind Mohammad
or a row of brown-cowled monks
with bell-&-gong,
or Satan (till the subject
tears away the God-helmet & screams)—

—Come
to Sudbury, to
The Dungeon, close
the five-hundred-pound steel door,
sit in the doctor's easy
chair & strap on the helmet,
watch the hung cross in strobe-
flash, hear the taped monkchants
& enter the temple, deep
in the temporal lobe,
the "minimally linguistic,
maximally affective"
seizures of the right amygdala,
enter into the brain's holy of holies. Come
Lord Jesus Christ, even now, come quickly, through electromagnetic
     pulse, &
rise for us out of the strobe.

(Good Friday, 2002)

THE LITTLE GLAND WHICH THE SPIRITS SURROUND

"Let us therefore take it that the soul

has its principal seat in that little gland
suspended among the cavities

in the innermost segment of the brain":

so René Descartes, 1649. Who chopped
the universe in two: cut

mind apart from matter—thinking-stuff from stuff-of-the-world—,
    core-split

twinned hemispheres like a pomegranate's, each
oozing its seedbursts. I think I think I think

& will be, without end. There's no place our soul so touches us,

Descartes says, as
in our cogitations. & where that thought-soul

interpenetrates nerve & vessel & striated

muscle & spinal wet
is only at this tiny,

teardrop-shaped bundle of pineal,

crusted with calcified brain-sand,
little gland

which the spirits surround:

Third Eye, penis cerebri,
"sphincter of thought,"

"natural pathway of chronobiology

caught between the psyche
and the soma"—

buried there, & staring.

X†X†

Where is the way
where light dwelleth,
Job asks,
& as for darkness, where is the place thereof?

> *And declare unto you that God is light*

Dwelling-place of photons' trace
in the nerve circuits, the filamental
spines of dendrites

from the eyes, rushed
tidings of dusk & rain-dimmed,
dwindled-to-nine-hour
days:

> *And declare unto you that God is photon,*
> *particle & not-particle, not-wave*
> *& wave*

—Brainlocked,

strung to the hypothalamus & retina,
that little gland
in its lightless cave,
secretive, & soul-secreting . . .

Because, like nothing else in the brain, it's nonduplicate, untwinned
Because it lies where the optic nerves
crisscross to the brain's back (chiasma
bearing light, light-   bearing
                              chiasma, crucifix
                                  or X)

—The first words of Yahweh:
Let there be light.
The last words of Victor Hugo: *I see*
black light. Word
to the pineal: suprachiasmatic
nucleus signing darkness,
rain, melatonin, sleep-
circuit, hibernal
issuance. Soul-
dormant.
The last words of Goethe's
soul: *Mehr licht. More light—*

Therefore that's where the soul
exercises its functions:
darkness-summoned, serotonin-
glutted, nonluminous

& preying on what radiance is ushered in . . .

MELANCHOLIA ORACLES: II

Inappetent,
benumbed: rage
firefly-sporadic & -dim. Sleep
jagged as surgical sutures.
Even sorrow hardened, unrecognizable, like the cherry tree's
stalactite amber sap, bee-burred & sterile.

JANUARY SLOUGH (SEVEN EXPOSURES)

The Brain has Corridors—surpassing
Material place—
DICKINSON

That desire should fail, by the willows there, where we lay down
our lyres

Lay down together without desire there, instruments
unstrung

   <<>>

Many-crevassed
surface, glacial
downslip of firn-pack

grim-lit, as if

skullbound, just behind the eyes.

   <<>>

The serotonergic
dawnlight

damped-out:
hammer-on-wire
in the dulled
medulla,

keys' muffled clink & thud,

replayed & replayed
D minor
etude, in deadened
vibrato: variation

without any theme.

   <<>>

Between the nerve-cells'
extremities

(because they can not touch)

the rift, the fissure, the slough, through
which the transmitters must be

fired

out of the synaptic cleft, re-
uptaken, that endless rocking
of serotonin, melatonin,
incoiling of self on Self . . .

   <<>>

That green in the kindling, that sopped rain
in the fibers of wood, that
smother-flame, quench & snuff . . .

   <<>>

Now the new year

sloughs its radiance
elsewhere, & here the light
dwindles, hoarded on slicks
of sleet-cling from gutters, & the hibernal
mind dims inward, staring outward as it slows

<<>>

—As Janus
gazes
through chained
gates (after, before)
toward the time
he can't get to
& the one he can't get beyond: only this

seized *not
yet, not
anymore, not
anymore, not
yet,* this

zero-exposure: ice-glued
colluvium
at the cliff's base, what's
settled there, what's
come at last to rest:

after-
creep, through the brain, the stilled moraine.

MELANCHOLIA ORACLES: III

Self-eradicant,
though my mind's
medicated now, & jazzed:
syncopated eighth notes, slurred chords,
backbeat, backbeat & drag.

LORD BRAIN

—Lord Brain, *Speech Disorders: Aphasia, Apraxia, and Agnosia* (1961)

O Seigneur, s'il y a un Seigneur, sauvez mon âme, si j'ai une âme
ERNEST RENAN

To see the universe
in a grain of sand,
in the scrunched
convolutions, a billion
synapses in a sand-
grain-sized speck
of cerebral cortex,
its cells immeasurably self-implicated.
Brain the size of two clenched fists.
Billion-grained mood in a grain
showeth His handiwork. Let
the meditations of my lobes
be acceptable in thy sight,
O Lord. Lord Brain,
canst thou not minister
to neurons wrongly wired. Agitations
of the hippocampus. O Lord
the brain secretes thought, Cabanis says,
as the liver does bile. *To see the universe*
marred in a billion billion-marred
grains.   —*Our cosmos*
is just one of those things that happen
from time to time, the physicist
said. Out of the unformed, & void.
Who can understand His errors?: alexia,

agraphia, amusia, allophones & vocables,
palilalia palilalia palilalia. Scrunches.
Neuron-spasms. Clenched fists. Speech
in perseveration, says Lord Brain,
is contaminated by words
the patient has already used
but cannot get rid of. Pointing
to scissors, the aphasiac said,
Of course that's not a nail file;
it's a nail file. Go to, let us
go down, & there confound
their language. & the Lord said
(Lord Brain, Lord Brain, canst thou
not minister) the problem
of speech has proved a highly
difficult one. Inflamed
encephalitic tissue's
testament: *What is what*
did you say did I say what
word is that word what
what do words the word what
mean. My brain secretes, Lord,
these slurs of supplication & lament.
& the mind secretes the idea of mind,
& the word *mind*, secretes
the cosmos that the mind is meant
to anatomize. *Just one of those things.*
Do not consult the gods
to find a directing soul,
Galen said: consult an anatomist. Lord Brain,
brainward I go, on the nerve-
impulse, the wave of negativity
in ions of calcium, voltage-

driven sodium channels
opening in the membranes, microcosmos
of synapse & dendrite. *Soma*
& *sema*, body & tomb. Antidepressants'
neurogenesis: let the dosed
cortex bring forth new cells, synapse
as all the space that's left of Chaos. & let
the neurons separate
light from darkness, exaltation
from despair, for days, & for years,
& so it was, & it was good, set
in the firmament
of the serotonin receptors on the dendrites . . .
Psyche's soma; sema's psyche. Lord
Brain, lately I don't know how to speak
again: mutism, speech-poverty,
introjection into the convolutions
& fissures where words get stuck.
Go to, let us go down, & there confound.
Sometimes, as you say, Lord Brain, the frontal-
lobe-damped can still sing
words they can no longer seem to speak.
& I meant to say: my life felt no more purposeful
than a paramecium's, or a slug's.
& I meant to say: all the spectra of light
our eyes can't even see—ultraviolet,
x-ray, infrared, gamma ray, heat—what
vision's diffracted among them,
unrealizable.
& what spectra of passions we can't feel, can't even feel
not feeling.
& I watched a slugtrail shimmer down the brick,
felt the dulling of my nerve-impulse, amygdala to cortex,

inchoate dread to thought-of-dread,
& I muttered, Lord, in the brain, Lord Brain, if soul there is,
if Lord there is, Lord, preserve
my soul, if soul
I have,
& I watched the lightning-bug larvae crawl all along that slugtrail
    toward their mucid prey.

THE DISCREDITED HYPOTHESIS OF TIRED LIGHT

The night sky's got no business going dark,
says Olbers's Paradox: an infinite

universe should be lit by some
star at every sight line, a hundred

thousand suns at every glance, in a uniform
luminosity so fierce it would boil

the oceans & scald away our eyes.
So the fact it's *ever* dark makes the cosmos

unplenumed, & the evening sky
punctuated by infinities of stars that just aren't there.

But I don't get it. Because I heard the light gets tired
& dims away before it grazes the globed

tunic of our eyes.
I heard the light gets tired

through all that ceaseless going: spent,
at six trillion miles a year,

toilworn & unmassed, corpuscular,
grit-thick with particles until it oscillates

in waves & waves away.
I heard it's been shedding its exhausted

force for fifteen billion years, so its redshift's
distorted, or that space-time's not stretched

thin after all, or that the Big Bang never banged, or even that time
began on the evening of October 23, 4004 BC.

I heard so many things my brain got tired.
But where does the light get to, when it sinks inside the eye,

& the fovea's electrons leap their levels & the light's
changed? When the photon gives its billions of years

of massless, chargeless, unslowable
power to the cones

so I can see, for just this instant, the slant-
shaft of cumulus-muffled,

rough-hewn granite trashbin out my window?
Undulant, & immaterial,

maxima & minima
of frequency & wavelength, crest & trough.

Billions of years, & still it can't slow down
but moves always so that distance is zero, so time's eternal,

& collapses to wave or particle only
when someone is there to watch,

quantum theory says: only when there's a brain in electro-
& chemical-rushings set off by photon

& optic nerve toward the back-brain's occipital lobes—
I still think the light is tired. Let it rest. Let the wave

function collapse, & the particle
function give in, let the drained & frazzled cosmos-wanderer

of light still
out of distance & into time, material & gritted & bound

to the worn, unparticled
convolutions of *now*.

COUNTEREARTH & LUX

(In Pythagorean cosmology, the nine spheres composed of the earth, sun, moon, fixed stars, & five known planets all orbited an invisible central fire. To bring the number of cosmic spheres up to ten—the divine number of completion & perfect harmony—the Pythagoreans invented a planet they called the Counterearth or antichthon, invisible from Earth because it followed our orbit exactly & shaded Earth from the central fire. The movement of the ten spheres through space made a music, inaudible to us only because of its familiarity, called the harmony of the spheres.)

FOR SUZANNE, AFTER TWENTY YEARS

Monad

•

A whole Earth's missing, Pythagoras says: though it turns
with us exactly, as the innermost sphere

harmonizing the music of its celestial passage
we can't hear only because we've always heard it,

inaudible in a deep accustoming.
We can't see it because it shadows us & lags our every move,

likeness unto likeness, & casts away
from us the central burning we're always orbiting,

twin & antitwin. He calls it
antichthon, Counterearth:

says it must be there to make the cosmos's
lyre-strings pluck, for *number is the measure*

of all things, & 10's the number of perfection,
being 1 & 2 & 3 & 4   26

combined: sum of the square; Divinity's figure.
If there must be 10 spheres, then 1 Earth's missing,

with its hum between us & luminance, its
consummation we can't know

we've always known. All things
are full of gods, Pythagoras says.

Dyad

.

. .

Every psyche has its music, its minor
version of the cosmic harmony, but warped

by the halved & skull-locked hemispheres of the brain
so it's atonal & unkeyed, its consonances warbling

away from the 10 spheres' music & into din . . .
For 20 years, Suzanne,

we've tuned those blues
together on a frequency only we

can hear, unearthly, a static
we've honed & honed into, grind

of spheres through the ether, the frictive
music of their common displacements

ours. 20 years we've convolved
in each other's occulted orbit

& the unknowable gravitation
of the other body has sung

into a common & echoing well.
So much alike we can only be

chthonic & antichthonic, 1 & 0, the isolate
& its recondite refusal to go alone.

Triad

.

. .

. . .

So the inner spheres
tune against each other

the music of their turning
around the unmoved cosmic hearth-fire, gone

in the eclipses of similitude,
analogue of occluded & requisite X.

Approximations of accomplished
desire: the light inside the light, the *lux*

imperceptibly lodged within the *lumen*.
In Augustine's optics the radiance we see—

what the receptors on the rods & cones cry out for—
is lumen, corporeal beam, the cosmos's

self-illuminant. But God's
in the light that lights that light:

the divine's the lux
inside the lumen, like the photon's soul, the way

the referent's in the word: charged & flitting,
there & not-there & there. Lux

is (you are) the vestige, sigil of the sign, re-splendence
of the splendid: insensible.

Tetraktys

```
            •
          •   •
        •   •   •
      •   •   •   •
```

If 1's a point, without dimensions, 2's
the first possible & necessary line, described

trajectory toward the missing other.
Always 2 points imply a linkage, & thus

the cosmography of form. Odd & odd are always even.

—If I speak of us in metaphor, Suzanne,

as metaphor, in the slippage of vehicle into tenor, in the implied

line between 2 points that have *no dimension, no property but
     location,*

as Pythagoras's 10, amplitude's assembled line & sealed
     circumference

(0 as antichthon: sphere that follows the singular & lifts it an order of
     magnitude),

it's because you move always beside me,
inside me, inarticulable, other side of the simile's *like* . . .

Because 20's the number of completion
added to itself, the way lux adds on to lumen

to make
not vision but a superflux of light, invisible gleam in the glint:

you the missing properties & dimensions,
lumen's lux, Earth's antichthon, singularity

& terminus, Suzanne: necessary & ever-incognita
terra, my point's point-of-arrival.

TWO

*wherein are
delineated the
species of hunger:
frogs consume
fireflies & thus
autoluminesce,
slugs consume
their own
genitalia, fireflies
consume each
other, & humans
devour Christ,
& brains swell
to consume the
world in song*

THE FULL SOUL LOATHETH AN HONEYCOMB;

BUT TO THE HUNGRY SOUL EVERY BITTER THING IS SWEET **PROVERBS 27:7**

HUNGER TRIPTYCH

(1)

At Eucharist, the server's
impatient & officious

hiss, as she points
toward the Host

still wrapped in my fist,
& holds the chalice

back despite
my consenting Amen:

*Please consume
Jesus,* she scolds me,

please consume Him first . . .

(2)

Autoluminosity
of the slimed frog? Its belly's

amber & green
matchstrikes through the underthroat's

vibrating croak:
in-lit with gut-

gleam, crouched
in the muck.

& a biologist
wild to capture

the first
bioluminous amphibian

till, deflated, he watched
the frog's

tongue-flicks
seize lightning bug

after lightning bug:
fireflies' glint-

stutter through the skin—scintillant, captured, from within.

(3)

So the convolute
intestine, the inner

feet of gut, jejunum
to cecum's

blind pouch.
Plato said its twistings

housed the mortal
& inferior

soul of the gut: lust-
issuer, glutton,

bound down in its manger
under the navel

like a wild beast, soul
of the soul's

hungers, one
of the parasitic

psyches that can't outlast its host.

VENERY

You must sit down, sayes Love, and taste my meat.
So I did sit and eat.
GEORGE HERBERT

For twenty minutes, at twilight, the male
lightning bug flits his mating flash
(*Love bade me welcome*)
a third-of-a-second glint, at two-second refrains—
semaphoric
flash-trains in the mown
stubble, learned
syntax of glint & delay,
hover & held gleam.

& the alien-
firefly female,
with barely a brain, has memorized
the precise reply of his species' females

(*quick-eyed Love*)
so she issues her imitated sentence
of answer, its
mating-yes, its *long flash & diminished glow*

        —Signal-mimic's
language of angstroms: wavelength, trough, & crest
Translated language of flash & pause, breed
& dupe
(language without brain)

& she lures him to her, where he hovers
from a leaf to pin
her wing cases for a ninety-second copulation—

               (*Yet my soul drew back*)
Then she seizes him instead, & sinks
her scythe-shaped mandibles
into his still-glittering belly
in the dark,

& eats.

MELANCHOLIA ORACLES: IV

In the cerebrum's
entrails—like the scrutinized
guts of sheep,
the liver's divulgent lobes—
the diviner reads the spelled-out
engravature of unease:

norepinephrine, dopamine, serotonin
dwindling in the synaptic gap, & with them dwindling
lust, hunger, relish, all
the species of beatitude—

In the amygdala, fingernail-sized
knob where dread
resides, with microelectric prods among
corrugations & infolds an inch inside the temple:
This spot
makes the subject lick his lips,
this spot, galvanic, releases a rage
no one knew was there
camouflaged in an island of gray matter,

releases
a shaking & baring of the teeth—

As in the liver's
forty-four zones, the augurs
once mapped out the cosmos
& the gods'
displeasures, in the swollen
lobes of Orion or Draco,
in the ill-
omened thickening of the gall.

SONG REGION

FOR MY SON

(1)

Begging's always the first song, pitched
to a shrill, as the syrinx of the hatched
songbird quivers toward the father's

craved beak. Then the rudiment-
music called *subsong*, rehearsal-trilled
through the nested canary's half-

sleep as its brain swells up to build
a neuronal house for song: *Higher
Vocal Center, Area X, Robustus*

Archistriatelis: their dendrites hyper-
stimulated by hormones & elongated
April daylight. But the stereotyped

mating song comes hard, syllables
practiced note by note for months.
The male canary has to learn how

not to individuate his song. He's got
to learn to trill the notes in shaped
& completely repeatable conformity

till the stereotyped
& mastered mating-
music settles down

at last into its unchangeable drone . . .

(2)

Melody-drained weekday, meaning-sapped,
after our cat's heat-yowl all night, gut-deep

—she's twenty, in dementia, not estrus, in
something-interior-consuming-her-body,

something no amount of feeding can feed.
& I'm back from lecturing on Genesis, on

how it was said *Let there be*, & there was, &
is, cat's beg-cry is, & the sense of all this

purposeless cadenza is, & is, the brain-
song's hunger for blues & croon, to sing

the day back into meaning, make it fruitful
& urge-ripe, & to call all that craving *good* . . .

Like Jin's blue water balloon we smashed
in rain, for its pure redundance of splatter

over his smeared blue chalk-word lessons
on the sidewalk: POP, SOB, ROT, GOD

—all the words with fat globes of lack
in their guts, so he'd remember them

because they build their shape from
waste & void . . .

(3)

Recitative & scat, recessional's
late spring lilt & trill. Till
midsummer molt, all breeding

done, when there's
a total absence of music
as the forebrain's song

regions molt too, neurons
disentangled & sloughed
off, shrunken nuclei

of Area X degrading
the song, its hard
syntax of mating

music unwired—& de-
known. That neuro-
eschaton as the useless

nerve cells of the learned
strain die off & flow
away in the bloodstream,

posthumous opus of the craved . . .

(4)

      —Sloughed
song-in-my-blood, & in Jin's
blood-not-mine,

adopted mine (I dreamed
before he came
I walked all over Seoul
begging the temples
to release him),

blood more my
own than my own, as the male
songbird trills to his half-
feathered brood the fed
music their brains
will adopt, note
by note, arrangements
of the desired
toward the desirer . . .

  .

(5)

Spring's end, dwindled nerves, & my
song's gone again, sung
up: song regions all synapse & no

runnels of warble & aria: no

praise songs in the shock-
to-shock & snatch
of serotonin in the neurons'
greedy receptors—

All's a slow molt in the solstice-glare:
shucked oyster shells & barnacle-crunch & glint
of beach-glass-shard in a boot-
stomp of wind-tough seawrack—

All's Jin, dragging
his skull-&-crossbones flag
& a long tail of sea kelp:
Look, Daddy, this looks
like a steeple t, he says, stretching
torn-off tendril over fat
tube of tendril, kelp
cross-shaped, t-shaped, salt-
water spangle
& drip—

All's Jin, leant over the walkway's
wasp-mound, staring
in, singing under his breath almost
in time with their out-
swarming *When I die*
Hallelujah by & by

       —All's
a slow molt & occult
regeneration into song.

HERMETIC ELEGY, WITH LULLABY

So you're gone

out of the diurnal, that urn
burnt & burnished,
unearthed again

& again—
Ground-
down cuneiform,
bejewelled & muddied

bone-cup: its relic-fragments
fit, almost, together
(into ossuary's
ash-spill):

pedestal & many-fractured arm.

o o o o o o o

Still, I drone you
sleep-stories at midday, midlife's

stutter: stuck-tongue

of the clock,
sundial in rain, the nursery's rhymes
brutish, inexhaustible:
Here is a candle, to light you to bed
Here is a chopper, to chop off your head

o o o o o o o

For no one at all, then, this monody:
diary
without days.

o o o o o o o

No One, my

melancholiac,
only now
dia-
gnosed (known-
apart)—you ·
of the ruptured
bile-duct
(*melas*: black; *khole*: bile),

internal
tear the surgeon can't seal shut again—:

o o o o o o o

Why should we need
this dirge, this
dug-up potsherd
to scrape, in ash, the sores, yours
(never-
allowed-
out
One)

& mine? *Melas*
khole, necrotic
shed Self inside . . .

oooooooo

The unsaid
is said now, won't be taken back. Won't
flow & reflux
between us anymore, like the estuary's
tidesuck & back-drag through eelgrass,

crab-drilled
mudflats, where fresh
current suffers its way into salt, & salt
spatters the still-fresh

gash of the rivermouth.

oooooooo

Is that your sleep-
breathing, that old
rattle & catch on each third
intake—

Why are you
interred, then?

oooooooo

Hum
with me your disallowance,

hum the hoarded
lullaby, the one
about not having to suck your fingers,
or shut your eyes

o o o o o o o

(*Child, thou nart a pilgrim byt & uncouth gest*)

o o o o o o o

Not having to rock, or break the bough

(so rigid
your kind of rest is) *Come*
slumber come

come   that bilious
& lulling old song
about not even having

gotten born.

MELANCHOLIA ORACLES: V

Self-
eradicant, in this craving
to be nowhere,
out of the way of my life, like a minimized
file at the bottom of the screen,
unobtrusive marker of the disappeared.

S

A *gigantism of the genitalia*
In the hermaphroditic
Banana slugs
On their slime bed on lichen
As the tentacles turn their
Long eyestems

Over the intertwined S'es
Of their bodies
& they gnaw

Away each other's tailpit's
Mucus plug, &
The breathing

Hole's upswollen by genital
Arousal as each casts
Forth a penis

Longer than its body
& for hour
On hour
The golden streaks of their slick
Forms tighten into a noose
As each
Penetrates sinuous each, as each
Gives & takes in
Sperm, & each's

Ova swell, fertilized. They lie still
For hours, then. So one
In the curled

Plural of their S that separation's
Near impossible: writhe &
  Lunge, the penetrant

  Genitals won't come loose until they each
Gnaw their own stuck
  Organ off, &

                Off. So this
            Is where we live. Is it somewhere
            Written that the radula's

                                25,000 teeth
                        Must slice across that mucid
                        Fastening, that the Earth

                    Must have these unloosed slits
                            Of slime plugs,
                                These egg-clutches

            Undersiding each leaf,
          Auto-amputations, these
            Glistenings through cut stems? Underfoot,

      Twisted in the fogbound ground,
        Dew-sopped against
          Desiccation. Lord,

    I must believe You know why
It—coil & slime trail &
  Barbarous

                            Disengagement & slick
                                Of eggs—must be—
                                Somewhere, un-

        Speakably pluraled—written into this our scheme.

THREE

*wherein the gaps
are filled, & the
full is emptied:
the soul's
atoms seethe
with quantum
fluctuations,
& the vacuum
spews forth
the cosmos,
& language
is smashed
to quanta, &
gluons loosen
in the brain,
& the brain
bristles with
its component
straw, & the
lord of the brain
is read in the
synaptic gap,
& the atoms
of unmeaning
assemble into
form*

THE ANSWER TO THE QUESTION OF WHY THERE IS SOMETHING RATHER THAN NOTHING

WOULD BE THAT 'NOTHING' IS UNSTABLE. **FRANK WILCZEK**

MELANCHOLIA ORACLES: VI

An end is come, the end is come, behold
now, see
it come:

Scythe-glint, its shock-light, through the hacked
rows of stubble.

oo-

oo-: *[prefix] egg; ovum*

I love the opalescent
roe-mass

of that globular
prefix,

little double
zero-glyph.

I love to mouth the sigh
& grunt of it, oh-

uh. An icon
of a man

clutching his jaw
in his hands

was one of the Mayan
forms for zero: posture

of abhorrence
or dismay. o

o, o
vum, o void,

milt-spill
at the freshwater's

58

source— So,
at the Big Bang,

the vacuum
somehow brought forth—

through a random
fluctuation of matter-wave

& antimatter particle—
everything there would ever come

to be, the "false vacuum"
seethed & spilled

zeroes & ruptured
eggs, in grunt & sigh,

spectacle
of vacua

& oosphere.
& that zero wraps

all around me
still, hands mashed to my jaw.

UNBEHOLD

Lord Nelson's hand, blasted
off by musket-fire at Tenerife,
stayed clutched into a fist

in the gap below his stump,
the unbeholdable
fingers stabbing

their ever-longer nails
into his palm. Daily
in the amputated place

the gone
fingers cut deeper
into the gone & welted

skin. If a hand
can outlast
its shearing-off & still

inflict its scratch & cramp,
he thought, how much
more must the soul

go on when the whole
body's a phantom
body, rid

of all but
its spirit's
fist-kinks & stabs?

THIS LIVING HAND

A strange? You'd call it a strange?
Yeh.
But it's a hand?
Yeh.

—Asomatognosia: rejected

ownership of a part of one's own body,
denied limb clung
somehow, alien, to the self:

When the stroke patient was asked,
Is this your hand?
Does it have another name?
She said, "it's a strange."

Why
mine, these half-drooped
lids & bulged veins,
dug-in hangnail & thrush-white tongue?
Why *mine* this lingual gyrus, this
substantia nigra—black
substance where dopamine's
held?

My father was the Circle of Willis,
little circuit of cerebral arteries
blocked, in him, by a single thrombus
thirty years ago, an
ailment not to be treated—

What flows in that circle now,
in his grave by the river in Macon?
What embalming fluid still drips through what shard of skull?

Every dream the hippocampus
& amygdala
haul back the memories they've hoarded,

in a frenzied criss-
cross of neural nets
(the six-columned
cortex abuzz with
the re-lived & never-
lived garble of story

& shocked-still freeze-frames):

Now my father is leaving his study
where he's been for thirty years;
he's leaving his grave-suit & wedding ring,
& he's sober now, as if
for the first time,
& he tells me, *Oh, I know where you live,*
it's magnificent there,
but still I don't know how you stand it, it's unbearably

replete with so many conflicting illusions . . .

Is he
mine, now, when he comes out of my mind?

                    See,
here he is, this living
hand, this
strange: I hold it towards you.   62

THE EXPLETION OF TAN

Tan. Tan. Paul Broca hunted our speech
down, in 1861, through its lack & toward

its fissure in a man who, since age twenty,
could say only *tan, tan, tan-tan, tan* & an

obscenity Broca never reported. Tan.
Expletive. Tan-tan. *A man Leborgne*

called Tan aphasic in a French clinic,
& when he died Broca saved his brain

in alcohol, & found tan tan expletive tan
it shrunken in the left lobes, & lesioned

from the Fissure of Sylvius to the Sulcus
of Roland. In its third convolution, a serum-

filled egg-sized depression, neurosyphilitic
locule. & around that fissure he found the brain's

clusters of language & speech.
& so Broca planted his name

on that region of speech, on that
brand of aphasia Broca's

Region Broca's
Aphasia (The Expletive of Tan-Tan).

Broca died of an aneuyrism in his brain ex
pletive & what did those fissures of Tan-Tan's

locution hold what triple
rhythms of tan what punc-

tations of pause between
that one shrunk syllable's

expletion of all other words
"The meaningless syllable

Tan" Medieval Latin *tannum*.
Tannin. Tanbark. Shredded

bark. Cortex: Latin for *bark*.
Bark of the brain's half-

stripped tree. In the Macon
Hospital, in the ICU,

I came from the Boy Scout
jamboree to see

my father, stroke-ridden,
for the last time & hear

his last words, not words
but a guttural

lung-deep when he heard
me speak his name, a grunt

that grew louder & more urgent
till I fled that room—

Now he calls me up, in sleep,
sometimes, & the operator-static

whistles *I am required by federal law*
to inform you you are receiving

a call from someone known
to be deceased, & I hear

that desperate-to-connect
bark again, that

gnarl of syllable
peeled off

its meaning & growing shriller
(Tan Tan   Tan Tan   Tan)

to carry off throat & glottis
& tongue what the left brain's

stripped bark knows, & doesn't
know how to tell it knows

—& I crush that phone in my hand.

THE SCARECROW'S SUPPLICATION

So the Wizard unfastened the Scarecrow's head . . . and mixed a cup
of cereal with pins and needles. Then he filled the top of the Scarecrow's
head with the mixture. . . . The Scarecrow decided to think. He thought
so hard that the pins and needles began to stick out of his brains.

L. FRANK BAUM, *THE WONDERFUL WIZARD OF OZ*

Tinman   hatchet-arm's   rustblotch
Monkeywings   dullgold brick's click & hiss

hiss of witchmelt   Poppydose, & doze
& everything emeralded, skywritten surrender

er   Broomstick in the grip. Crushed
rubyslippers under the ripped-up

stormcellar's cement rootstock   she said
aunt'sface in the cornstalks, in the seeall

witches' glass   Crow on crow on crow on crow
unscared in a field It watched over

I It   alphabethalves   Secondhalf only
O through Z   Oz   Havenot   Stuff

ing through rainworn seams   Backstuck pole
Untraversable   desertspread between Kansas

& SouthWitch what
slipper's heelclick

what luffed balloontether
& green ribs of Ozthrone   66

what housewhirl
or match struck

to straw or lionclaw
or hammerheads' smack & flatten

what goldstep's thousand days
skull-gives

& headwithin
go thinkings straw-to-straw-to-straw

to needlepin eyesbehind not a neuron not a synapse not a white
matter not a convolution not an

an   not an *a* through an *n*
Oz's   needlestore, & straw's needles   Roost-crows on straw   .

To be afraid   to speak Dorothy's
To speak Dorothy's unwitchwords   Come

Come back   *w*
itch

izard in
aw

bra
str

Brainstraw   Take back
these needles, Ozlord   O-through-Z   need dulls

headstuff & stab
if that's all the brain   you can give

MELANCHOLIA ORACLES: VII

Three-pounded
meatslab—

Even mirth, when it returns—Effexor's
first jerking through the nerves—
feels leaden, discontinuous
from the rest of the self, like a prosthetic limb.

The pleasure receptors
reassigned now, to the urgent
business of self-blame:

electric
linkup, signalling
mea culpa, mea culpa, mea
maxima culpa
spiking in every crevice of the brain.

THE ATOMS OF UNMEANING

Democritus, the Laughing Philosopher,
denied any purpose in the clash
of atom against atom,

in the patterns of their
hooks & barbs
as they snatch & disattach

into goatskin, Aegean surfwrack:
the thorned atoms of fire
& the smooth-grained

soul atoms. To know
that lust & grief & pleasure & dread
come only from the world's atoms

bumping randomly at the atoms of the soul
is to be freed of all heaviness,
Democritus said, & to live

in continuous bliss
amid the unmeaning
agitation of fire-thorn

toward globed
soul-grain, atom-
hook to void-barb, freed of significance: so, laughing.

SOUL ATOMS

Are not five sparrows sold for two farthings, and not one of them is
forgotten before God? But even the very hairs of your head are numbered.
Fear not therefore: ye are of more value than many sparrows.
LUKE 12:6-8

The fall of every sparrow—it is written
that He watches, in cattails & salt marsh,

black streaks in the flank, wing-coverts & burnt
umber plumes. & He watches, too, the electron-

cloud of each disintegrant atom
& all the assembled syllables

of the suicide note as it's written
(*I used to have a heart*—she wrote—*I have*

something which beats now in its place)
& sees the shed electrons in the left

hemisphere's language folds that think those words,
& the brain stem's coordination of her scribbled

The sun, the Earth, & the very stars do not
exist, & the surge of potassium to calcium

from nerve cell to nerve cell, uncharged to un-
charged waves of mind in volts of negativity:

those quarks, too, He watches, He must watch.
& so the aurora's iridescent blast

in waves of solar wind over Lake Superior
August night, dissembling over tidepools

of water striders & blackfly swarms
into eruptions & inswarmings &

inside-out tunnelings of ionosphere,
photon-storms in coronas of backlit

quantum leaps in atoms of oxygen:
I watched Him watch me

watch those face-shaped
surges of green & stutter

to tell Him of Dickinson's
"Of Bronze—& Blaze" & of

His own *Unconcern so sovereign
to Universe, or me—* . . . On my back

on moss-slick cliffside, I'd been thinking
all night of Madame Zero, who called herself *It*,

having no self anymore to name
(*All is dead within & outside It*)

who believed she wandered the vacuum,
the only matter-remnant of the Big Bang,

a carbonized star, even time itself
annihilated, so her *abysses*

of dejection could never end . . .
Under the aurora's unfoldings

& infoldings of the implicate
& arcane orders. He heard her saying

I have no stomach, no intestines, no
heart, & now He watches me read the lamplit

pages of *Pathologies of Belief*
as the soul atoms oscillate & bump,

sideswipe one another & impinge
(like the water striders' tense skitter

at each vibration of the jag-
rock-bound surface of their pool—). Like neutrinos

the soul's atoms penetrate everything,
omnipresent & imperceptible

& all-permeable particle-rain.
& the molecules of Effexor

permeate even them—C_{17}
$H_{27}NO_2HCl$

into the depressive brain's
noradrenaline & serotonin,

its synaptic reuptake's snatching-back
of the molecules out of which it hews

pleasure. Unconcern so sovereign
to Universe, or It—Madame Zero,

of the case-studied *organic disconnect*
of the sensorium from the limbic

system's emotion-of-being-alive
so feels sometimes the universe to me:

& I think of particle accelerators
hurling their leptons into light-speed

concussive disarrangements of any
fundament the cosmos has ever unveiled

& I dream of that one collision that might
annihilate all the universe's

matter accidentally one weekday
morning, & I can't stop wondering if

some gist of things would somehow last
if everything

were gone in one instantaneous
turning-back of matter into the force

it came from, & all capacity
for knowing any of it had ever been—

history, space-time, language, us,
the aurora's boil & seethe & retinas

that snag & upend its image in packets
of photons—were dissolved, in the twinkling

of an eye, without even a trumpet: *how*
would it matter, I keep thinking, & to whom?

Lord of unmeant & meant, Lord of galaxies
elliptical & dwarfed & overscattered

through space-time's fifteen-billion-year hyper-
repulsion from the first matter-giving

blast: even the incalculable swarms
of bacilli secreting their slime-layers

to ooze through my gut—even them You number,
every flagellum they wave. & the three-

hundred million sperm set loose in each
lovemaking. With what amusement or revulsion

do You watch the ion channels open,
sodium pumps set to work as dopamine

receptors fling those molecules
back into the gap one forty-thousandth

of a millimeter wide, that synaptic
no-place where Your kingdom is finally

come? I am to a bacterium, Lord,
as the entire cosmos is to me,

as an Effexor molecule is
to the soul it slashcuts. You watch, strange

God watch with me now
the sparrow's unnesting & flutter-fall

to ground, Madame Zero's pilgrimage
through the burnt-out universe in her mind,

soul atoms' inertial slow adjustment
to dimethylamino

methoxybenzy
cyclohexanol hydrochloride

in the sealed-in inner cosmos, in
the brain's screened-of-contaminants blood.

APHASIC ECHOLALIA

Lord if soul if Lord if soul preserve
If preserve consume Please consume
Jesus please consume Him saved in
Alcohol in brine the offal of the skull
Secretive & innermost thinking-stuff
Stuff-of-the-world I see black light
Hover & held gleam in the lightless
Brain-cave no center into which it *could*
Collapse   A strange I call it a strange
Lord replete with so many conflicting illusions
If soul there is in the amputated place an ailment
Not to be treated preserve if Lord there is if soul there
Is in its resident fissure its lack Consume Him please consume Him
Where is the way (where the light dwelleth) & the dwelling
Place of darkness who will find it Lord caught here
Between the psyche & the soma amid the unmeaning
Agitation if soul there is among the cavities in the innermost the
    light that lights
That light If gut there is the vacuum seethes & spills amid the
    convolutions
Please a strange I call it a strange unbearably replete What do words
The Word what mean garble of story & shocked-still freeze
Frame so many conflicting illusions If soul there is if Lord
If soul there is seized by tongue-flicks Sloughed song-
In-the-blood I see black light if black light if
Lord there is lust-giver jellyfish-mucid
Unbeholdable not-particle
Not wave preserve me
Let me consume
Thee brain-
Locked
Lord   76

MELANCHOLIA ORACLES: VIII

Once more among morphemes,
syllables, the stilled
dwelling of the migrators,
unutterable slowness of the always-inchoate words:

Brain waves glide
faster than light,
they used to think: faster
than any force in the cosmos

till they timed the impulses'
halt & delay, indwelling
stall.

When thinking
is jammed shut:
hinge-screak, latch & knob's
rust-crumble. Smell
of something long-dead behind that door.

PARTICLE ACCELERATOR

Apo   apo   apophasis

Endo-logue, the numen-dom

Dys-logos   nulli-morph

Re re re re Non

Apo apo apo Logos apo non
Dictus counter sensus, counter scriptus,
apodictus,
theos vox ruptura,
theos
Ex.

x
glossa omni gnosis
Linguacosm. Sembl- -script. Psyche-
locu-
chasm

= Hyper-
phasis

                    + + +

—If I came toward you instead in the speech of a catechism,
    interrogative
& sure . . .

+ + +

Meson lepton baryon:
micro-telos.   Quan-
tum: in-fin-
i-tes-
i-
mal:
(*Quantum*
which means: *How great—*)

Mega-nano

+ + +

Apotheos fractus dictus dicho-logos

Neo
X. Crux, neo re, neo
Non. Lux. Laud & lau-
gh.

Q: What is the soul
A: The soul is a living
Being, without a body

Oo-ego
Corpus-less

Onto- ecto- Logos Endo-sum

Anti-nucleo-
centro
Fide- -phon

Dys-theo-
graph-ia

Logos, khristos, fractus. Via
vacua. Sacr- -nym.

PHASE TRANSITION

When the gluon bindings loosen, the quarks

can swim free,
the physicist said: when the gold-on-gold,

light-speed-smashed
together nuclei dis-

integrate, at a trillion degrees,
in the Relativistic Heavy Ion

Collider on Long Island, oh gold's

protons melt into plasmic drip

(the newspaper says) like
millionths of a second after the Big Bang . . .

& the dream's Inquisitor probed me: *What is mass?*
I fumbled, blank, palms

to my temples, & all I could think
to murmur was $E=mc^2$?

& he shook his head, his hooded eyes
downcast: *You don't know what Mass is, do you, you don't even know* . . .

* * *

I know that mass is radiance ensnared
& frozen down into form

because the universe outrupted so far it chilled
& clotted—

I know there's a heaviness called the God
Particle, the Higgs

Field through which all matter
has to shove its way;

it snags & downdrags everything
that's not unglued into light

& that's what makes this June morning
—possum's litter-trail of boiled peanut shells

& cantaloupe rind from the compost,
bindweed tangle in honeysuckle,

phone pole shadow on rose trellis—
feel so deliberate, so slow—inertia's

its only face. Power
debilitated into matter, that's what mass is.

* * *

Something's loose

this summer, in my brain,
as though the mind's
gluons kept coming
apart, the brain cell's nuclei
like a plasma of melted-down quarks

in-collapsing,
aboriginal & gummed-together & inutile
for thought—

* * *

One night the dream says God's
macrocosm is a hundred thousand years:

any space-time less than that is imperceptible
in the Kingdom of Heaven,

as quarks are to us, as superstrings are:
aeons on aeons God sees, but human history's

microcosmic to Him, merely
theoretical, just beginning

(like the gluon-quark plasma to us, like the Higgs)
to agitate its way into view.

* * *

If the Higgs

Field could be stripped away,
we'd all be particulate & enwaved,

in light-speed-vanishing, no assemblage into mass
or matter,

incapable of any interaction
(trampling down

death by death)—
Because mass is a body's only

resistance to acceleration
(and the root of Mass

is *to send away, to throw—*)

—Loosen

the gluons, Lord, gold-on-gold colliding, disassemble
me, boson by lepton,

nerve-spine by axon's hillock,
dis-

miss me, send me away (unto ages
of ages), strip

me down into whatever Mass is, massless, let me go . . .

MELANCHOLIA ORACLES: IX

God-of-the-Gaps,
the cosmologists call you,

God made up, shard by shard,
to give some name to what we can't yet know:

space-time's
ellipse, dark energy, dark matter,
antigravity ripping the universe apart—

God of slowed synapse & undecodeable brain-spark,
God of the aboriginal
vacuum filled somehow from the beginning with quarks, God
of the lightning bug's sexual flare, the dung beetle's dig,
groundhornets' heaped temples on the walkway,

a slug's glossed slip down the bedroom wall,

I feel your long-gone succor

again, sometimes—
axon to dendrite, serotonin
receptors atwitch again—
as it moves through the synaptic gaps, the clefts

—& I call that tempering
you, God-
of-the-Gaps, abeyant one,

neuron by shocked neuron,
I call it You.

PHANTOM LIMBS OF THE POEMS

wherein the reader's brain is spared from molten disintegration amidst the convolutions of the black-lit language of quantum mechanics, neurobiology, & psychocosmology

Brain Slices

The *cortex* or *cerebral cortex*, measuring an eighth of an inch thick, covers the top of the brain and controls most conscious thought.

Photons are particles of light.

Gyri and *sulci* are convolutions and furrows, respectively, on the surface of the brain.

If Religious Beliefs Are Simply Neurocognitive Processes That Reduce Anxiety Concerning the Dissolution of the Sense of Self

Transtemporal: In neurology, meaning "across the temporal lobe," which is the part of the brain just behind the ears involved with sound, speech comprehension, and some aspects of memory; in theology, meaning "across time" or "interpenetrating time from eternity."

The amygdala is an almond-sized brain structure deeply tied to emotion, especially anxiety, anger, and fear.

Out of the mute / right brain: The left hemisphere of the brain ordinarily processes language (speech, comprehension, reading, writing); Persinger hypothesizes that the right brain, not having access to language, creates nonlinguistic visual and emotional images when electrically stimulated, and that the left brain's language centers then interpret those images as mystical presences.

Come / Lord Jesus Christ, even now, come quickly alludes to Revelation 22:20, "Amen. Come, Lord Jesus," the next-to-last verse in the Bible.

The Little Gland Which the Spirits Surround

"Where is the way where light dwelleth . . . " is from Job 38:19; "And declare unto you that God is light" is from 1 John 1:5. Light and matter both manifest themselves sometimes as particles, sometimes as waves—the famous particle-wave duality in which paradoxically they appear to partake of two very opposite natures at the same time. This duality is one of the things that led physicist Richard Feynman to say, "I hope you can accept Nature as she is—absurd."

Dendrites are the receiving ends of brain cells, through which signals are taken from the *axons*—or transmitting ends—of adjoining cells.

The hypothalamus is a pea-sized structure in the center of the brain that controls hunger, thirst, sexual desire, and other basic drives.

The suprachiasmatic nucleus regulates circadian rhythms—wakefulness and sleep in synch with daily cycles of daylight and night.

Melatonin and *serotonin* are chemical neurotransmitters that are involved in regulation of mood; melatonin release is triggered by darkness.

Lord Brain

Sir Walter Russell Brain, later Lord Brain (1895–1966), was one of the leading British neuroscientists of the twentieth century.

This poem relies on frequent allusions, especially to the creation stories in Genesis 1 and 2 and the story of the Tower of Babel ("Go to, let us go down, and there confound their language" in Genesis 11:7). Shakespeare's Macbeth asks "Canst thou not minister to a mind diseased, or pluck from the heart a rooted sorrow?" Blake's "To see the universe in a grain of sand/And heaven in a wildflower" moves through the poem. "The firmament showeth His handiwork" and "Let the meditations of my heart be acceptable in thy sight" are from Psalm 19. Physicist Edward Tryon remarked that "the universe may be just one of those things that happen from time to time."

Many of the technical terms on disorders of language are from Lord Brain's book *Speech Disorders*. *Alexia, agraphia, amusia* are, respectively, disturbances to the ability to read, write, and recognize melodies. *Palilalia* is repetition of a word or phrase. *Perseveration* refers to involuntary, uncontrollable repetition of words or phrases.

Wave of negativity/in ions of calcium . . . : Nerve impulses are conducted through the brain cells by way of electrochemical waves in the negatively charged ions of calcium and sodium in the brain. No one has yet fully explained how such electrical disturbances get translated into conscious thoughts, sensations, and emotions.

Antidepressants'/neurogenesis: Recent research suggests that antidepressants work partly by triggering new brain cell growth (neurogenesis) in the hippocampus; see, for example, "Requirement of Hippocampal Neurogenesis for Behavior Effects of Antidepressants," *Science* (August 8, 2003): 805–9.

Mutism and *speech-poverty* refer to the flatness and dulling of speech and the decreased sensation of "having anything to say" during depression.

& I watched the lightning-bug larvae crawl all along that slugtrail toward their mucid prey: Is there anything more chthonic or earthbound than slugs? Is there anything more ethereal than fireflies? Larval fireflies prey on slugs, as the inchoate soul feeds off the things of the flesh.

The Discredited Hypothesis of Tired Light

Olbers's Paradox asks why the night sky should ever be dark when the light of billions upon billions of stars is traveling toward Earth from every direction.

Tired light, first proposed in the 1920s, was the idea that light loses energy as it travels over vast cosmic distances and so can't be seen by the time it reaches us.

Time / began on the evening of October 23, 4004 BC: In 1650
Archbishop James Usher calculated from an extensive study of Biblical
chronology that God must have created the earth on this date.

Let the wave / function collapse: In quantum physics, the "collapse of
the wave function" refers to the moment of observation of a subatomic
phenomenon, in which the range of possible occurrences (the "wave
function") "collapses" into the one occurrence that is observed. Reality
is sometimes said to have no objective existence until the moment
of observation collapses the wave function and reduces the multiple
possibilities to the one actuality that is observed to occur.

Counterearth & Lux

Monad, dyad, triad, and *tetraktys* are the Pythagorean terms for one,
two, three, and four, which together add up to the holy perfection of
the number ten. A visual representation of the points of those four
numbers forms the equilateral triangle known as the Tetraktys:

$$\begin{matrix} & & \bullet & & \\ & \bullet & & \bullet & \\ \bullet & & \bullet & & \bullet \\ \end{matrix}$$

$$\bullet \quad \bullet \quad \bullet \quad \bullet$$

Lux and *lumen*: "*Lux* was God-given, essential light, the being of
light, and as such a reflection of its Maker. Augustine viewed it as
the simplest, noblest, most mobile and diverse of all corporeal being.
Lumen, by contrast, was the material means by which our perception
of the being of light (as *lux)* arose. When we sense the brilliance of
the sun, we are perceiving its *lux*, but we do so by unseen *lumen* that
connect it to us. Between the time of Augustine and Galileo, the being
of light that ensouled space (*lux*) retreated, leaving behind its hard
material vestige (*lumen*) as a fossil record." —Arthur Zajonc, *Catching
the Light*

Hunger Triptych

Jejunum / to cecum's / blind pouch: Jejunum and cecum are sections of the intestines, where Plato located the "soul of the gut."

Venery

The title, from the Latin *venus* for love or *vener* for hunt, is an archaic word meaning either "indulgence in or pursuit of sexual activity" or "the act, art, or sport of hunting; the chase."

Song Region

Higher / Vocal Center, Area X, Robustus / Archistriatelis: Three regions in the brain of the canary that grow new brain cells to accommodate song-learning during mating season and then shed those nerve cells into the blood when the mating season is over and the song is forgotten.

Neuroeschaton: Opposite of "Lord Brain"'s "neurogenesis"; *eschaton* refers to the end of things, the last things, time of destruction rather than creation.

Hermetic Elegy, with Lullaby

Child, thou nart a pilgrim byt & uncouth gest (translation: Child, thou art but a pilgrim and an uncouth guest) is from a medieval lullaby.

oo-

oosphere: an egg ready for fertilization

In many versions of quantum cosmology, the universe is thought to have emerged spontaneously and without cause from the primordial vacuum, by way of quantum fluctuations in the texture of the vacuum.

Hence, *vacua and oosphere*: the universe in a zero state of the vacuum as an unaccountably fertilized egg.

This Living Hand

The poem alludes to Keats's fragment beginning "This living hand, now warm and capable" and ending "see here it is— / I hold it towards you."

Melancholia Oracles: VII

Effexor is an antidepressant medication.

Soul Atoms

Quarks are the constituent particles that combine to form the nucleus of the atom; *leptons* are subatomic particles including the electron, neutrino, and muon.

The poem deals with a neurological condition known as Cotard's Delusion, in which the patient becomes convinced that he or she has died and cannot be convinced otherwise. Madame Zero's story is told in the book *Pathologies of Belief*, edited by Max Coltheart and Martin Davies.

Emily Dickinson's poem "Of Bronze—and Blaze—" concerns the aurora borealis, or northern lights, and includes the lines "An Unconcern so sovereign / To Universe, or me— / Infects my simple spirit / With Taints of Majesty—."

Effexor, whose chemical structure is identified twice in the poem ($C_{17}H_{27}NO_2HCl$ and "dimethylamino methoxybenzy . . .") works on the neurotransmitter *norepinephrine*, which is involved in the regulation of mood.

Particle Accelerator

Particle accelerators are vast machines that propel subnuclear particles to enormous speeds and energies, smashing them together to force them to surrender even smaller particles. This poem is conceived as a language-smasher, breaking words into their cognates and recombining them into new particles.

Apophasis (etymologically, "away from speech") refers to an approach toward God through negation rather than affirmation; saying what God is *not* rather than what God *is*. This so-called "via negativa" or negative way toward the divine relies on a language of negation rather than on one of assertion, since God is seen to be utterly beyond the capacities of ordinary language to describe.

Phase Transition

A "phase transition" is the passage of matter into a different state, as when water remains H_2O but is transformed from liquid water to ice, or from liquid water to steam.

Quarks, the constituent particles that make up neutrons and protons in the nuclei of atoms, are held together by particles called— appropriately—"gluons." Recent experiments have succeeded in producing a phase transition in protons in which, for the first time since the Big Bang, their quarks and gluons have melted down into a primordial soup known as a "quark-gluon plasma."

The Higgs boson, a theoretically predicted particle dubbed the "God Particle" by Leon Lederman in his book by that name, is thought to form an all-pervasive field throughout the universe; objects are believed to have mass to the extent that they interact with the Higgs field.

Trampling down death by death and *unto ages of ages* are phrases from the Orthodox liturgy of St. John Chrysostrom.

THE CONTEMPORARY POETRY SERIES

EDITED BY PAUL ZIMMER

Dannie Abse, *One-Legged on Ice*
Susan Astor, *Dame*
Gerald Barrax, *An Audience of One*
Tony Connor, *New and Selected Poems*
Franz Douskey, *Rowing Across the Dark*
Lynn Emanuel, *Hotel Fiesta*
John Engels, *Vivaldi in Early Fall*
John Engels, *Weather-Fear: New and Selected Poems, 1958–1982*
Brendan Galvin, *Atlantic Flyway*
Brendan Galvin, *Winter Oysters*
Michael Heffernan, *The Cry of Oliver Hardy*
Michael Heffernan, *To the Wreakers of Havoc*
Conrad Hilberry, *The Moon Seen as a Slice of Pineapple*
X. J. Kennedy, *Cross Ties*
Caroline Knox, *The House Party*
Gary Margolis, *The Day We Still Stand Here*
Michael Pettit, *American Light*
Bin Ramke, *White Monkeys*
J. W. Rivers, *Proud and on My Feet*
Laurie Sheck, *Amaranth*
Myra Sklarew, *The Science of Goodbyes*
Marcia Southwick, *The Night Won't Save Anyone*
Mary Swander, *Succession*
Bruce Weigl, *The Monkey Wars*
Paul Zarzyski, *The Make-Up of Ice*

THE CONTEMPORARY POETRY SERIES

EDITED BY BIN RAMKE

Mary Jo Bang, *The Downstream Extremity of the Isle of Swans*
J. T. Barbarese, *New Science*
J. T. Barbarese, *Under the Blue Moon*
Bruce Beasley, *Lord Brain*
Cal Bedient, *The Violence of the Morning*
Stephanie Brown, *Allegory of the Supermarket*

Laynie Browne, *Drawing of a Swan Before Memory*
Oni Buchanan, *What Animal*
Scott Cairns, *Figures for the Ghost*
Scott Cairns, *The Translation of Babel*
Julie Carr, *Mead: An Epithalamion*
Richard Chess, *Tekiah*
Richard Cole, *The Glass Children*
Martha Collins, *A History of a Small Life on a Windy Planet*
Martin Corless-Smith, *Of Piscator*
Christopher Davis, *The Patriot*
Juan Delgado, *Green Web*
Jennifer K. Dick, *Fluorescence*
Wayne Dodd, *Echoes of the Unspoken*
Wayne Dodd, *Sometimes Music Rises*
Joseph Duemer, *Customs*
Candice Favilla, *Cups*
Casey Finch, *Harming Others*
Norman Finkelstein, *Restless Messengers*
Dennis Finnell, *Belovèd Beast*
Dennis Finnell, *The Gauguin Answer Sheet*
Karen Fish, *The Cedar Canoe*
Albert Goldbarth, *Heaven and Earth: A Cosmology*
Pamela Gross, *Birds of the Night Sky/Stars of the Field*
Kathleen Halme, *Every Substance Clothed*
Jonathan Holden, *American Gothic*
Paul Hoover, *Viridian*
Tung-Hui Hu, *The Book of Motion*
Austin Hummell, *The Fugitive Kind*
Claudia Keelan, *The Secularist*
Sally Keith, *Dwelling Song*
Maurice Kilwein Guevara, *Postmortem*
Joanna Klink, *They Are Sleeping*
Caroline Knox, *To Newfoundland*
Steve Kronen, *Empirical Evidence*
Patrick Lawler, *A Drowning Man Is Never Tall Enough*
Sydney Lea, *No Sign*
Jeanne Lebow, *The Outlaw James Copeland and the Champion-Belted Empress*
Phillis Levin, *Temples and Fields*

Timothy Liu, *Of Thee I Sing*
Rachel Loden, *Hotel Imperium*
Gary Margolis, *Falling Awake*
Tod Marshall, *Dare Say*
Joshua McKinney, *Saunter*
Mark McMorris, *The Black Reeds*
Mark McMorris, *The Blaze of the Poui*
Laura Mullen, *After I Was Dead*
Jacqueline Osherow, *Conversations with Survivors*
Jacqueline Osherow, *Looking for Angels in New York*
Tracy Philpot, *Incorrect Distances*
Paisley Rekdal, *A Crash of Rhinos*
Donald Revell, *The Gaza of Winter*
Andy Robbins, *The Very Thought of You*
Martha Ronk, *Desire in L.A.*
Martha Ronk, *Eyetrouble*
Tessa Rumsey, *Assembling the Shepherd*
Peter Sacks, *O Wheel*
Aleda Shirley, *Chinese Architecture*
Pamela Stewart, *The Red Window*
Susan Stewart, *The Hive*
Donna Stonecipher, *The Reservoir*
Terese Svoboda, *All Aberration*
Terese Svoboda, *Mere Mortals*
Sam Truitt, *Vertical Elegies 5: The Section*
Lee Upton, *Approximate Darling*
Lee Upton, *Civilian Histories*
Arthur Vogelsang, *Twentieth Century Women*
Sidney Wade, *Empty Sleeves*
Liz Waldner, *Dark Would (The Missing Person)*
Marjorie Welish, *Casting Sequences*
Susan Wheeler, *Bag 'o' Diamonds*
C. D. Wright, *String Light*
Katayoon Zandvakili, *Deer Table Legs*
Andrew Zawacki, *By Reason of Breakings*